Author photo by   L. Steinbach

Published in the United States by   Fence Books
                                        303 East Eighth Street, #B1
                                        New York, NY 10009
                                        www.fencebooks.com

Book design by   Rebecca Wolff

Fence Books are distributed by   University Press of New England
                                        www.upne.com

and printed in Canada by   Westcan Printing Group
                                        www.westcanpg.com

Library of Congress Cataloguing in Publication Data
        Brenner, Daniel [1976–]
        The Stupefying Flashbulbs/ Daniel Brenner

Library of Congress Control Number: 2005938750

ISBN 0-9771064-3-8

FIRST EDITION

THE STUPEFY-ING FLASH-BULBS

DANIEL BRENNER

THE STUPEFY-ING FLASH-BULBS

CONTENTS

PART 1

PART 2

PART
3

PART
1

LIQUEFIED

I went to the whirlpool and asked it
N it looked at me & said child of the sea
Listen as I tell U of the child of the earth

The child got stuck up and hibernated
N started crying
Said the letter N on a lonely hill
Shut up I said it's just the wind

I went to the whirlpool and asked it
N it looked at me & said child of blood
Listen as I tell U of the blood of ancestors
N it was mixed with birds

APPLE WASHER

Fraud the whirlpool is a fraud
We are in the weeds about it
Lurking around in thickets
Through which we have cut
Great swaths and made them
Roads with chemicals and buried
The chemicals in alcohol
That we poured out on the road

I asked the whirlpool the other day
& it came up with a reliable answer again
& it was early comparatively
I finally got to say
No nothing like that the horse is the only 1
Who knows the answer n
They are done drinking

ANCESTRAL SUPERHERO

I went up to the whirlpool and asked it
How does it catch fire in the air then how does it
& the whirlpool said that it swam in fire
& then suddenly I was crying in the sun
Surrounded by plants
The children in armies
Are fighting the ancestral monster
In flash superhero zodiacs

It's too vague I said to the whirlpool
But it reminded me of having a blackout
& it was okay from before when I told it to shut up
Well I tell the whirlpool the poor lions
Deserve I get to then it cuts in says I know best

MACHINES

There were machines mainly
He had a machine too it was green
We congregated and then it called out
I strolled out
Going back in I noticed that the machines
Had learned to walk up n down stairs
So we took pictures of them with the other machines
And slept with our eyes open
Because it was easy for them to sneak up on us
The machines slid down the stairwells
At odd angles & we were not just
A play-set machine in a thunderstorm

WHIRLPOOL AND NON-OBEISANCE

The whirlpool said that I never wrote this
With a pen just as a fact
But I took it like a problem
What whirlpool at it again
Yes whirlpool says through April & May
Thru rain & sunshine
I am twisting like a spire
Very interesting I said
That about says it then I got nervous
Gesture magnetize what we do
I asked the whirlpool finally what we do
N a vase fell off the shelf and broke
So I went n told the whirlpool
Oops up make me a drink

THE CUBE

It whirled around the Phoenicians
Too like their robotic speeches
Chasing current events around
& the hid with cupboard recipes
Freedom is so much
So when the lasso comes say
You and me
The three of you & we will go to sea
Together
After the revolving doorway
Where it all comes from
The whirlpool
Spun by what spins the cube

CUBE AWES CENTRAL ELECTRIC EYE
BY THE LIGHT OF THE MOON

The cube of evil provided an impetus
For those who stole it like me
They took it away with cranes
And threw mixed metaphors at it
I'm stuck
I don't want help no
Just to close my eyes and continue
Turn around into distant provisions

METAL SPHERE

The evil cube has turned into a metal sphere
With the face of McLight who lived 2 towns over
In the beach tunnels of our consumer dreams
I'm sure of it this time we all have them
But who cares about the evil sphere or cube
When u are in the middle of the bay
Through all the confusing wind and water

The evil cube has turned into a metal sphere
That rotates containing yellow light
Before splashing down into the stomach
So that u have to draw in the thin air
I know it's unpleasant but the roots are
Stable at least lower down the air is more
Curative there
Through that which all you are ha-ha invading with spite
For protection
As the word-rate increases and spiteful cross-eyed smoke
Abhorrence
But snow in the garden anyway
21 screaming interruptions from the shovel people
With their egregious apologies scattered toys &
Wait no more like 22
I was wrong just counting cars

THE PHOENICIANS DISCUSS

The Phoenicians discuss whether to greet
The whirlpool or get up in the stirrups about it
Wreathed in flowers
Shame on the lions for fooling us
Seal up the sun with putty
The weavers will not go
They will sit home brightening doorways
The tree is still there

MCLIGHT POTTERY

I missed some of the pottery
When McLight was talking about blur
Because of the boats but they stopped me
& said that I was trifling with
The chain n the sea leopard
Of the square view limited by ships and horses
Into loop rides of groovy McLight pottery
Carved with scrolling mantras & aquatic life

It is a 21st century thing that emerged from the
Phoenicians long ago in the underground sea
Where pills of McLight float in the greamy sea
Hoping to influence trains n such to confess
For all the time it's still a diminishing option
Down ancient lines into myths or 2 be ridden
About the prophecy when it gets slalomy

SEVERITY

The cube returned and it made me nervous
You too I see & yet you read on
Recovering a sense of blurry theft
Recovering or so you thought
It's raining out
The cube is out there waiting
Tagged by dreams & ½ as strong
Like a romantic spider jacket
A Korean smoke boat
I keep the cube in my apartment now
In the cage in my crib
With the porphin and aces
& my lizard skull helmet
In a house in a tree
Under the bridge
Under the carpet
Mysterious and vexing
In the wooden structure
Tagged and waiting for the electric impulse
That Susan is going to give it
And then
It will be time to lean right

POSTURING

OK so maybe the cube was just my way of posturing
On a black wall and smoking a red cigarette
Lanes but there are new bruises forming believe me
There are new stories coming with relation to these
Cubes and spheres with the face of metal on them
Within a new frame smirk-smirk a new nickname

But you know that the cube is Phoenician
& as far as the face she might as well be McLight
Because we all face the terror of the scream
The Phoenicians developed in the days of wood cubes
Skip it
It's just more distant dissonance
The main goal is still to rock and appear extra-excited

DEW

The cube has become dusk to dawn
Artificial and the reels keep going on with
Abhorrent fancies so this silence to it now
The plasma helmet and everything else
The whirling blob and the six-blink cube
We may whirl around into an attack move
U never know specious blame is in the cards
Along with waxy hubcaps boats sewers
Gardens spiders and jewelry
You are protected by the chaff
Or at the least a wig and costume
Just like you are mingling with them
Looking for maxims from them
For the wheelbarrow trip home
To the playground of remorse
With silence and scratched photos

RATHER INTO MCLIGHT

The cube waits for no one
But in time there is balance
Stolen and snow covered
Greaming
Everlasting and pinned
Reversed and stapled by shovel people
Stamped and dotted in popular song
It's only convention
I hiss that to you as a secret
Here in the woods where none can hear
We shall make the inner world
To match the cube of the globe
& maybe still have time to try skiing
McLight is a cube of night
A soft scream by our trailing leaders
A nether nothing silver car implosion
Green bottle rush from the courageous hay roof
The Phoenicians built

GOODBYE MCGILL

McGill of the metal sphere
I am in the chlorine room
With the noxious fumes
Reading like a nice person
They turned up the heat
So I say goodbye
Yo puma
And dip the book in a vat
Then I go to get a snack
This is no way to be down McGill
It's like a song somehow

IRON PLANK

Hey-hey-hey we built a death ray
And a bird to match the Phoenicians
We're fucking hypocrites
Hey-hey on the train
We're just passing by
Later we might turn up missing
Hey-hey-hey we built a death ray
In the library
& the horizon goes click
As the wheel clicks into place

THERE IS SOME ORANGE SODA LEFT THOUGH

McGill got mad when she found out that I made her
The metal sphere with her face on it instead of
Something cuter but I twirled my moustache and said
Your youth McGill that is all I am capturing
With horrorscopes and mad delinquent rushes

Stop the clutter said McGill no more like whined
So I stopped and said here then is your apple
Hoping to avoid whatever would come next
The interruption or the mold or whatever McGill
Remembered as being particularly abhorrent

Maybe the decay of premonition or plastic instead of
Gold or unconditional awareness or acceptance
Of decay is more noble for us robotic beasts towering
In our houses taking pictures of sunsets and
Pumping rounds into the silent animals

Everyone should know for now that in hindsight
It's special vengeance
Because we can sweep it into a corner anyway I conclude
I said goodbye already remember
By the river?

Well at least I'm not the cube of evil said McGill
But I said don't be so sure it's abhorrent in relation
To foreign art clusters that are stolen just the same
In neon butterflies fluorescent tubes n hummingbirds
OK u cornered me I admitted but was out of apples

THE CUBE IS JUST A BILLBOARD NOW

I created a cube of pure evil
& encouraged others to steal it
Word spread about it
I think it might have been translated
In a bunch of mirrors in a
Trend setting kind of handshake way
The stars were interested at least
Sitting up on their footstools of power
In the evil cube's dynamics
& deceptive distances

Well I'm sure you're bored by now
What he's saying he created it you say
Well I know it was the Phoenicians
You're right it wasn't me

The Phoenicians scribbled it down
On worn water-rocks
& I stole it from them
Huddled in the mist and foam
Crouching on a nest of eggs
Near the mountain path
Where the cube fizzled out wind-fleas
And cathode-ized its tents & leaf-piles

SELF-INFLUENCING

The cube of evil has drawn sycophants
From far and wide to gaze on McGill
In the mirrors of the metal sphere
McLight shoots from their fingertips
Shoes are still the most important thing

They approach her with influential
Sanguine-green gunnery
The first mention of McLight
Comes in Phoenician dimensions
She opens her satchel of youth
In the fountain town without screaming

I stole the cube from the Phoenicians
Huddled in tree vapor as in a ground fog
Reversing the buildings of my youth
And leaping onto the light transfer
Obviously we are re-involved in it
Parallel to each other
By the west side stadium she is spitting poison
Saying I didn't really tell you that

She did
We were separated by a tunnel
It was before they changed colors
There were wildcat stalks
Connecting us
It gets blurry here
Invasion is help for protection
I'm taxed with the discovery
The cube has gone on vacation in the tropics

SETTING

I had no premonitions about the west side stadium
Just kidding the stadiums paced in dreams
Everything was very badly lit whatever that means
They say they say
I know I see a concert there in the future sometime
Or a monster truck show or something
I'm not claiming credit after all for it
It's someone else who told me
She walks in the bad lighting near the stadium
In my premonitions
She is smiling
She walks beside the stadium
Along train tracks

THE WHIRLPOOL

I am the whirlpool of glass
With the flask because I am
Also the snail & lettuce
I am so blue liquid
Please McHandbag s
I have 2 eyes
Instead of filtration
I am the den
I am moistened
I am Mr.
Mr. McEye I have 2 eyes
Where the flavors are
And instead of filtering
The lions & flowers
I have filth left the knight
Fills the electric bridge
Where the lions bleed
Tingling leaves of the moon
The furnace is no less modern
We are doomed
We spliced a lot together
And fuming electric choler
The new wake up
The right lights wake me up at night
We have another do something no one
Do what when class 10 uses fire
The horse needs abuse for stuttering
It is not really good all the time
After which comes the worm

PART
2

CALLS FOR MORE SODA

It's boring more orange soda
I am on Eagle Ave. looking for more
I am on the tiny crystals u put under tho
It's boring and so much like
The brass knobs rattle
Like Hessians to the tune of sirens into the
Houseplant

I'm sorry it's so boring
I try to be cool but
All those artists in the destroyer
I am just a thief

ROCK LION

Twitch drumming
Trails off
Stop dreaming it's good
Fast & leave
Hop-less & fresh
The sweet-shop
House forgives effigy
Weaver disaster
Eagle sandwiches
Blurred bubble letters
Ragged animal tracks
Light up the right
Makeup night stair
True but not
Like it went sphere square
Instead of sphere spiral

INTERCOM

Please avoid the war bell and get zooted
Help the nurses as much as possible
What's with the water
Let's laugh all the way back to the cave
Of snow carrying our war karma ornaments

This part is in sleep code but memory's off
The comic-books already know about it
Dear Veronica the horses' feet bump this is
American cinema on doomsday
The background extortion and drudgery

HORNS

It's like a torture because
I'd rather be brain-dead
With vanity plates
I don't know what else to do
Look at all this soap
It's probably because I'm sick
Look at this jungle oasis
There aren't even any lanes
Look at this gutter candle
I take to the swap-meet
I'm not real anxious to freeze
I'd really rather not discover all that

SEASON'S SONGS

The season's songs see
If the shovel people were serious
About the dream or waking up
How would they do anything
But migrate in panic
Not being like statues
Everyone was interested

I know the swamp breaks your compass
With the bells and tattlers here
In the ranch house or Cadillac
& it looks like California
I thought all I have to do
Is stretch a little and listen
To the mice nibble

STRAWBERRY CHIP

Please accept this fake arts-and-crafts sampler
With the theme of rattlesnakes rattlesnakes
The bishop eats his jaws are like them
Bring do bring rescue will he won't he
Revving into absolute red is easy before
The small dead chivalry bird accident
It is clear where the lawn starts by now
Never the victim of outrageous fortune
3 hoarse and weary adventurers or 6 cats
Orange ones with the real crimes that led us
To make new endeavors like these for the
Cognizant stapling of the sleep materiel

SLIP

Swanky congratulations everyone must
The last 1/3 was be so proud u are right
It should be out but instead it is half or
Making the 3 kinds or following along
Trying to be such an echo like a swath

Or smiling admonition here on the Nile R.
Which we are watching inalterably
The real running goes on at the very top
Of the pyramid where the air is deafening
& Looped over by the selfish weeping victims

SILENT REGARD

There are always contradictions to ketchup
But in chips there is the
I said why it hurt me
He says I don't know that animal but I'm
Blind and the animal says I see u whistle
So they all run out in the street talking large
About how Xi An got all that & all is 3past
Little bit but I don't care about windows
I'm just a stupid pig who smashes the lamp
In a pen built by capitalists
Who is next
Why
(MW) fish
I know
What a fickle alliance

STAR-CROSSED SALVAGE

He swims in dreams shielded
By ink with tickets
He is dark-dark and there is
Fire in the air

One of them will disobey
First at the first way
Which clay will first fly
Who will work & provide

They are going to crash him like hooks
After his ten minutes but faith
The vogue repetition is formulaic
& a mistake was made back there

ANTHEM BAG

Outside the mall the wind howled
The air was that purple feel
The wind did what
Seriously
It was almost evening
The wheel spun and fire
Came out of the rocks
A bird was there
So was I
The store beckoned to us
& a plate of corn chips
On the sidewalks on the 21st
Of Vienna they forgot grammar
& got down to it like
Movie stars
Different from ordinary people
Let's tattle-tale
Because it means nothing
Isn't that what we think

HERE IS A JUMP ROPE AND SOME ICE CREAM

The interviewer asked my mentor
If he had made anything up
This was before the engine burned up
With the patterns in it
But anyway during that moment
He was a role model and he
Told the interviewer no I didn't
Make anything up while throwing
A paper airplane

QUOTE UNQUOTE PISSING YOU OFF

Like, like, like, like, like . . .
I know what does it
Passing notes in class
Crying
Ruining my dreams
Mocking my name
Asking questions
Acting all suspicious
Using the made-up words
Snow spiking the crickets
Saying just friends
Rolling the dice
I'm a oh then you're a

AUTHENTIC TIC

I remember never going back
Ill fed and silent three years ago
I was hungry and authentic
Silent dissimilating & paranoid

I got my certificate now
I can be more playful
We are both cowards after all
The reason is confusing
Or at least that's my impression

SATELLITE PHOTOGRAPHY

Justice
We're caught up here in the express train
Under flickering lights
With triptychs
Suggesting that there were way more than 2 answers
To REMEMBER THE BEACH?

(Pause)

Speaking of that the way they were singing to me
It became apparent that some of the awareness was justified
It's time to put the cloth on the cage
& avoid
The stupefying flashbulbs

DREAMSONG

Rock some macaroni
Snarl at that stuff
Sunny day that stuff bad day
Have some tea alarm goes off
Central mystery
Fire
N the wardens say
Fiddle dee dee
Fiddle dee dee
Fiddle dee dee
Fidelity horticulture
Fiddle dee dee
Well riddle me this
Fiddle dee dee
Inciner de egregious

KNIGHT AT DAWN

The knight sat up on his horse n said,
"I am so tired and weary
although we both know how to love,"
(clown drops mirror)
"Clown dropping the mirror,"
(people nod off)
"People noddin off,"
(wait a sec)
"Excuse me,"
the knight said,
"I am speaking here;
I know how to love,"
(nods off)

& the maiden suffered
with the songs of terror

TIDE

Make a stand
It's time 2
Go to the zoo
Like I was telling U
For years
The 1 thing
U believe

& she says
I'm talking fuzzy
Yeah yeah
It's what I'm
Talking about
& she says
The detta chain

PARADE

The invisible knight
Ripped the visor
From his helmet
& looked askance
At a windmill
Covered in poisonous berries

SUNSETS TOO

Solid enough to care
Steal everything I hear
& claim them after all
This why those
Sink-posts get me tickets
What would u do
If u were never me
Chores or lies
Or un & another ritual
That is why I have hope
That I/you are un/an
& ancient like a ritual
I don't know how to do
In all the fake sand

STOP SCREAMING AND START SCRATCHING

The wind-up car just flips over on peace
I know what I need to keep flipping
I know what it means I don't know
The sky goes up in fire
Just for a few months
Only to cease when the sharpness
Makes me look up in a dark room
What is the question mark doing
Or not doing there

NATURALLY

I play a Dutch boy on paint
It is an arc sodium trip
Light not sound
The feud of the fire
Axioms and actions
Electric blue one too
I don't know sleeping bolo
Moth plum orange stars
Too cold not hot OK
Me I say w/unnatural things

NAPALMED BIRDCAGE

The oxidized ashtrays totter
Bubblegum for dinner
Artist of the year
Mayor Bossanova
Ponce de Leon
Raked apart with demon claws
Radiator
Mirror gray
Baseball leader
Rosa wasn't there
So neither was SJB
Wood & ashes
Watch-cog philosophy
Running targets
Framed in three
At the Sichuan place

ROLL OVER

I am not a memory politico
Suddenly feeling successful
She roared on the boat
When she scented the smoke
I had plans of the boat in my head
My friend was making it
Or maybe it was a bridge
We shared on pumas
Or built real bridges
I forgot about the boat
The TV said good night Carter
Y ultra that cool sea air

ENGINE

Everyone watches TV in
The living room w/ hollow eyes
Her thumbnail paint is exquisite
I said I want to tell a good story
About her but I said ghost story

She didn't say anything
In fact wound up in a field
Where nothing grew but then
The shore came in & we took something
Weather burning grotto birdsong

WHERE ARE WE

There are no beans anymore
Everything in a glowing ball
Rolling down the street to me
At night when the neon is lit
At the parties where their guests
Laugh & talk about sailing
Tanned striding from tree to tree
Escaping to the lowest point

CLUE

No pictures here or music
Burning daily & key twirls
But no music plenty to drink
Footstools no sorry no floors
Nothing to say to the shovel people
To rely on them for new colors
Or languages or beatings
No secret weapons here or
Typewriters or sidewinders
Or Ube
Just virtue I promise
I swear
I'm still on your side

BUILDING AN ANGLE FLUME

:eoa///
:eoa ear,iffs
lot
laaaaay.
There.
Black
Cat
Head
Cod
Called
Champagne
Stairs
Amber
Not
Arc
Collapse
Definitive
Two
Start cap
Blew out parents doors
What they said
Head rocking 2s
Ahead
Crass man
Elevate
I am
Oh
DE
DE

PART
3

INVISIBLE PROMISE, INVISIBLE
CONDIMENT

Backwards machine this morning's
Incidences in the afterlife
Dream-life made me parade
Drove me to all that stuff
I misappropriated & catch phrase

Hooded skeleton in a cage by the river
Something missing
It goes to the seashore
Offers lilacs
Takes them down from the sky
Out of the clouds
Builds a dam in the rain

A magician can capture it
With a twitch of his sleeve sit down
& imbue insight
The audience's kisses are for the creator
Collar me to that power

NO GHOSTS IN DEVIL'S LAWNMOWER

Down from the island was a bridge
It floated on the water
Shorts
King of the fake viands
The fake fortune teller
W/ the roads filled up
The lamplight on water
Filthy secret rusty chain
Falling chandelier
Short of the mark I never
Accent of water flow 2
Quiet the burner it's ok
Pg. 1: it was torn
Phones of course
Rain goes down the sink
Wait a minute I don't know
I didn't hear a thing
Airplane engine 2 loud
Yes I am guessing a #
Between 1 & double snowman
Horse or arrds are
It's turquoise and sand

SAI SILON

A new hat for the statue excellent
I have the perfect idea the perfect idea
I think I know what it means at this point
The kid says something on the hardwood floor
It is about alcohol again pans and pans of it or motor

Chemicals which could be radioactive
We all believe it turns into an animal a cat when it
Sleeps with the 2nd god the god it believes in
It comes eventually anyway you might as well accept
When it comes with the banging of pots & pans too
Perhaps it is better that way than any other way

I grow them in the rearview now
It doesn't matter anymore what they are finally
A photograph flashes by covered in heat & pain
So grow up on it with them like a camera
No this is not that I meant
I was not in the slide or Chicago

WEIRD EVIL

What goes on when your eye
Marches to the music of bones
Can you erase the movement
Can you convince them that
The plateau above sensation is fine

Half of your face melts away
For the generations
To sterilize in the rain
Abandoned chunks of hair
& elemental misunderstandings
Into the original human void
Where it just screams in the temple
4 seconds

WONDER ROCKET 1840

Whither ist the square man who reads of diamond mines
& is smashed down by the nonsense & lies in his soul
Into the bars of branding zoo thieves who call Wonder Ms
The one that is too quick to slip thru shovel people hands

Sometimes the haze is so bad I am biting at the rest doubled
Down by the river where the apples fall with the hail under
The wreathed swamp figures the ones with sage plastered
All over the muck and seed and condyle caught in their hearts

BEACH PELICAN

What you threw those two or three times
Broke after you breathed them and changed
Waves on the beach or above where the
Scrub of the shore appears the grass is
You could say that the net is
In a kooky camp-house sort of way
That everything is anyway
Even the iron gate leading back
Past the eyeballs of reality
During the infant thing when the insects
It was earlier than school when they
Or something about the moon and a train
Red leather accoutrements dark night water

TAPS ON THE PLUMBLINE

I can't get the carp to start
It's too abstract
Giles made the balloon
The nun is in error
<drop   taxi

Spackle man was dully
Tying Giles on like weight
Out of honor out of duty
His walkman rattled on
Audible to the hall monitor

Loyalty arrived for tea
Jaunty but we were all asleep
Her bird has called me
But
It is just a lost cry in nowhere land

Fax me the phonetics by noon
& we will put on a show
For the spiritualists
About how it really is

Halt let me see your taxi license
Let me see your tiger
Listen to the tiger sleeping

QUINTESSENCE

Houses and highways underwater & moss
Coming out of the fortune teller's dead body
Visions or rather ice cream in the sky
Meow I know I swum up to the road so it's
Blink smoke get it away from the mouse
Squeaky clean where I rolled
Rusted clunk gutter-ball sooner than it appears

Listening when it is a dream is a puzzle the wind
Might say as in reality like a cloud I awaken
The sprinkler goes off everyone is bored at this
Rattling someone hears a bee in the woods
Homing in on that single butter cookie probably
Or the number you closed the book on like an accelerant
A wrestling with a footstool & spilled rainwater

GRAVEYARD WAVIER

I tried to tell everyone how I broke
All of their candle-holders
Because of the wind but they weren't
Buying

Finally it's so boring to talk about
Let's hope it remains in the shelled
Onions of these last cries

Close your eyes & look around
Etymology of around
Lots of ways to make

A dish of crumbs
The Hessian's dialogue
Cut into a little ribbon with a heart
We don't have to respect them

FASCINATED SINGER

In their plumage on your stoop
Contagious
After the wreck the phoenix starts
Anew mesmerizing
Meanwhile on Mt. Storm
The thunder king rolls around
With his flintlocks
All we owe is allegiance cartoon
Karpesi sarpeum
A paragon to the death
Of holding godheads hostage

I see you thief in the heart of heaven
Is this right bad man
Very pretty

LADDER

Edge sunset rain garbage drawer flame
Better voices to inform me
Surrounded by coup counters
That communal bathroom
In the bathroom I thought about
Someone said the other day about
Stop
They'll congratulate you for something incomplete
Blundering on
I know the war hurts sweetie
That registers better days as being increasingly
Hallucinations the recipient
In a barn by the side of the road somewhere cluttered
In the mirror it's silver
A narcissist's rainbow
The hesitant present
Horse coats and blinders

COVERED

The terrified river heads disappeared
In the explosion or two
The radioactivity seemed into
Something else
Manna tablets
Speeding cars & fiction subs
Ice takes it all out
Ex covered in the winter trees
Shards of disappointment &
Falling down the stairs about art
The boys at the lake are wrong
At the mall it's Texas vs. arcade
A hypnosis of sorrow
Upside-down

LOLLIPOP

In the morning we said some things
In the afternoon
We practiced rhyming them
Yeah-yeah
The primers are full of dumb squared dreams
& the covers are down with spinning games
Flattery is conventional
Like a trope that dances down the street
I can thump along that now echoing
20 + 45 + 20-odd satellites
All doing the same flashy simpering
What a piece of satellite
Did you see his blazer
Get the dunk tank ready

FROSTING AND ANEURYSM

Fake eyelashes
So much damage the tint knob snapped
Fire rings instead of smoke rings
Becoming negative space again
Lots of crying and some glowing
Harpies perched on elephants
Ferns dangling from organic ceilings
Everything is ready now
A sign falls over throwing up salt
One wonders whether I am there at all
On Nougat Rd.
In spangles of jelly
Moving like ice
On the relegated art form
Bent on code words
Standing on Styrofoam
In the center of the river

CAT'S EYE

Metal everywhere & evil silver
With the heart in her lion and noble
She enters the sun infrared easily
The canes they say deeper me too
I am the one across the years now
So my loss that I was just like see
Or stuck over with all the stickers
Or drunk or serious about the cart
EJ kid is up on cement blocks w/
P grappling since you followed my
Camera directions & power trips
Can I not forgive 2 and the stone lion
Wu thing from the amorphous
Group I am in cupidity under the sun
I don't care what right n wrong is
One Dec. everything but wait
2 out of 12 or 10 of the set doorway
Star in wanted posters
Add your own wasteful cries
Your loud imperial orders for
More blazing wings and feathers

OUR LANE LEADER

Our lane leader is blue and we cry to him in books
Cool she's back from the unicorns I thought &
I saw her in the hillside heel-deep in a gore slough
Puzzled beside the car in Germany cursing at the light
As I tried to hold 3 umbrellas above (Aliens crackle)
The star-maker stable-master who pours a 2-liter bottle
The restaurant check-out wheels spin out alienation
Spies sulk nearby trying out their acting gigs
The cadre's oncoming lights & Spanish horses
The vampire girls are everywhere in the gore slough
They are everywhere the ponies bristle at their food
They are on the nation in soaring clusters around
Our lane leader blue like the pills lazy mommies take
Glhao up fa the dark leader ½ roared get to work
& all of his UZI followers flickered in and out of wanting
Those three cinnamon things flickering out there
In front of the cables with the bittersweet cool

SAVAGE COMFORT

The statements were twisted complimentary invective
It all goes back to dreams of tall cages crawled across
Fractures
A mocking burial there
In the key of braggarts
Technicolor salt mine
Oh but don't we get stuck revisiting for most of it
It's like when you want to leave but instead wind up working
Actually it's sort of the opposite
It's more likely autumn
It's rotten because it's right

Do you have dreams where the drama kicks in
& do you ever wonder about being a playwright in a swimming pool
Because it's about having the wiles to make it my fault
Isn't it

Then the people who mess with you write a song about it
We all make mistakes
I'm afraid of looking back from the perspective of being chased
& doing whatever it is that the perspective of being chased urges

Fence Books is an extension of **FENCE**, a biannual journal of poetry, fiction, art, and criticism that has a mission to redefine the terms of accessibility by publishing challenging writing distinguished by idiosyncrasy and intelligence rather than by allegiance with camps, schools, or cliques. It is part of our press's mission to support writers who might otherwise have difficulty being recognized because their work doesn't answer to either the mainstream or to recognizable modes of experimentation.

The Alberta Prize is an annual series administered by Fence Books in collaboration with the Alberta duPont Bonsal Foundation. The Alberta Prize offers publication of a first or second book of poems by a woman, as well as a five thousand dollar cash prize.

Our second prize series is the **Fence Modern Poets Series.** This contest is open to poets of either gender and at any stage of career, and offers a one thousand dollar cash prize in addition to book publication.

For more information about either prize, visit **www.fencebooks.com**, or send an SASE to: Fence Books/[Name of Prize], 303 East Eighth Street, #B1, New York, New York, 10009.

For more about **FENCE**, visit **www.fencemag.com**.

FENCE BOOKS TITLES

THE ALBERTA PRIZE

Practice, Restraint	Laura Sims
A Magic Book	Sasha Steensen
Sky Girl	Rosemary Griggs
The Real Moon of Poetry and Other Poems	Tina Celona
Zirconia	Chelsey Minnis

FENCE MODERN POETS SERIES

The Stupefying Flashbulbs	Daniel Brenner, judge Rebecca Wolff
Povel	Geraldine Kim, judge Forrest Gander
The Opening Question	Prageeta Sharma, judge Peter Gizzi
Apprehend	Elizabeth Robinson, judge Ann Lauterbach
The Red Bird	Joyelle McSweeney, judge Allen Grossman

FREE CHOICE

Yes, Master	Michael Earl Craig
Swallows	Martin Corless-Smith
Folding Ruler Star	Aaron Kunin
The Commandrine and Other Poems	Joyelle McSweeney
Macular Hole	Catherine Wagner
Nota	Martin Corless-Smith
Father of Noise	Anthony McCann
Can You Relax in My House	Michael Earl Craig
Miss America	Catherine Wagner